◆FOCUS◆
Reading for Success

Hop, Skip, and Jump

PROGRAM AUTHORS
Richard L. Allington
Ronald L. Cramer
Patricia M. Cunningham
G. Yvonne Pérez
Constance Frazier Robinson
Robert J. Tierney

PROGRAM CONSULTANTS
Bernadine J. Bolden
Ann Hall
Sylvia M. Lee
Dolores Perez
Jo Ann Wong

CRITIC READERS
Maria P. Barela
Phinnize J. Brown
Jean C. Carter
Nancy Peterson
Nancy Welsh
Kay Williams

John C. Manning, *Instructional Consultant*

SCOTT, FORESMAN AND COMPANY
Editorial Offices: Glenview, Illinois

Regional Sales Offices: Palo Alto, California •
Tucker, Georgia • Glenview, Illinois •
Oakland, New Jersey • Dallas, Texas

ACKNOWLEDGMENTS

Text

"Seeds" from *Cricket in a Thicket* by Aileen Fisher (New York: Charles Scribner's Sons, 1963). Copyright © 1963 by Aileen Fisher. Reprinted by permission of the author.

"The Animal Song," author unknown, appears in *An Arkful of Animals* by William Cole. Boston: Houghton Mifflin Company, 1978, p. 75.

Photographs

Pages 72–73: Raymond F. Hillstrom; Pages 108–109: Tom Bledsoe; Page 110: Jeff Foott; Page 111: Leonard Lee Rue III; Page 112: Jeff Foott; Page 113: Jeff Foott/Bruce Coleman; Page 114: Yellowstone National Park/National Park Service; Page 115: Galen Rowell; Pages 124–125: M. Philip Kahl; Page 126: Wolfgang Bayer; Page 127: Milt and Joan Mann/Cameramann International; Page 128: Suen-O Lindblad/Photo Researchers; Page 129: Wolfgang Bayer; Page 130: David C. Fritts; Page 131: David C. Fritts; Page 132: Wolfgang Bayer; Page 149 (top): *Are You My Mother?* by P. D. Eastman. Beginner Books, 1960; Page 149 (bottom): *Just Like Daddy* by Frank Asch. Prentice-Hall, 1981

Artists

Aitchison, Ed 140; Allert, Kathy 133–139; Brooks, Nan 102–105; Connelly, Gwen 56–63, 86–94, 95–101; Craig, John 22–23, 70–71, 106, 141–142; Eberbach, Andrea 38–49; Hockerman, Dennis 24–31, 32–37; Jordan, Laurie 116–123; Koch, Carl 150–158; Loccisano, Karen 8–15, 16–21; Mitchell, Kurt 50; Randstrom, Susan 51–54; Rosenheim, Cindy 81–84; Scott, Jerry 143–148; Wilson, Ann 64–69; Wilson, Don 7, 55, 107

Freelance Photographs

David Arndt 74–79, 80, 81 (bottom) 85; Ryan Roessler 149

Cover Artist

Kurt Mitchell

ISBN 0-673-21006-5

Contents

Stories By:

Sallie Runck

Mary Shuter

Lisa Eisenberg

Mary Anne Magnan

Section One
Helping Out

I Can Help

Come Out, Puppy

One day Carol said, "I have a
puppy.
Come and play with my puppy."

Bob and Rosa ran with Carol to
play with the puppy.

Carol said, "My puppy is in the
puppy house.

"Come out here, Socks.
Bob and Rosa want to play with
you.
Come out, like a good puppy.

"I can not get Socks to come out."

Bob said, "I'll help you get the
puppy out.
I'll give the puppy some water.

"Come and get the water, Socks.
Socks, come out here.

"Socks will not come out to get
the water."

Rosa said, "I'll help you get the
puppy out.
Socks will want to come out and
play with the mouse.

"Here is your mouse, Socks.
Do you want to play with it?"

Socks saw the mouse.

Socks ran out to get the mouse.

Bob said, "Your puppy is a big
one, Carol."

Carol said, "Socks, do not jump on Rosa."

Rosa said, "Socks likes the mouse."

Carol said, "And Socks likes you and Bob."

Help Find the Bear

One day Billy said, "This is a
good day to play with my bear.
I'll get my little yellow bear."

Billy ran to the table.

Billy said, "I put my bear on the
table.
But my bear is not here.
I want my bear."

Billy saw Mike.

Billy said, "Mike, I can not find
my bear.
Will you help find it?"

Mike said, "I'll help you, Billy.
I saw the bear in your room one
day."

Mike and Billy ran to the room.

Mike said, "I do not see the
bear in this room."

Billy said, "Carol likes my bear.
Carol will want to help find it."

Mike and Billy ran to see Carol.

Billy said, "Carol, I can not find
my bear.
Is it out here?"

Carol said, "I do not see your
bear, Billy.
But one day I saw it in the puppy
house."

Billy ran to the puppy house.

Billy said, "I see the mouse in
here, Carol.
But I do not see my bear."

Carol said, "I want to
help you find your bear, Billy.
But I have to keep my puppy in
the water."

Mike said, "Billy, the puppy has a
bear in the water."

Billy said, "Is the bear in the
water a yellow one?"

Mike said, "It is a yellow bear.
I'll get it, Billy."

Billy saw the bear.

Billy said, "It is my bear.
Come here, bear.
This is a good day.
I have my little yellow bear."

Just for You

You can make a bear like this one.

1. Get this.

2. Make this

3. Do this.

4. Do this.

5. Do this.

A Job to Do

BE *joyful*
IN HOPE,
patient
IN TROUBLE,
AND
persistent
IN PRAYER.

ROMANS 12:12

Jobs
Ken - Frog Helper
Sam - Room Cleanup
Beth - Plant Helper

LIEN ELEMENTARY SCHOOL
469 Minneapolis Avenue
Amery, Wisconsin 54001

The Frog Likes to Jump

Ken has a job.
The job is to give the frog clean
water.
But the frog likes to jump.
The frog jumps out.

Beth has a job.

The job is to water the plant.

Beth puts some water into a pail.

The frog sees the pail.

The frog likes to jump.

The frog jumps into the pail.

Beth said, "I can help you, Ken.
The frog is in this pail.
I'll keep the frog in here.
You get water for the frog."

Ken said, "Good, Beth.
I'll get the water."

But the frog likes to jump.
The frog jumps from the pail to
the plant.
Beth runs to the plant.

But the frog likes to jump.
The frog jumps from the plant to
the table.
Beth runs to the table.

Ken asked, "Do you see the fly on
the plant, Beth?
The frog will want to eat the fly."

Beth said, "I'll get a pail.
I'll put the pail on the frog."

Beth and Ken run to the
plant with the pail.

The frog sees the fly.
The frog jumps from the
table to the plant.
The frog eats the fly.

Beth puts the pail on the frog.

Beth said, "The frog is in here."

Ken said, "Good job, Beth.
I'll get the frog from the
pail and put it into the water.
The frog will like the clean
water."

What Is in the Hat?

One day Mr. Grant asked, "Sam,
will you help?
This room is not clean.
I want the boys and girls to
help clean the room."

Sam asked, "Will this hat help?
You can put jobs into the hat.
The boys and girls can take the
jobs from the hat."

Mr. Grant put jobs into the hat.

Judy saw Sam with the hat.

Judy asked, "What is in the
hat, Sam?"

Sam said, "The hat has jobs in it.
You can take a job from the
hat and help Mr. Grant."

Judy said, "I'll take a job."

Sam asked, "What is your job?"

Judy said, "My job is to clean the table."

Sam said, "Mr. Grant will like a clean table."

Judy said, "I'll get a pail and some water."

Judy ran to get a pail and water.

Daniel saw Sam with the hat.

Daniel asked, "What is in the
hat?"

Sam said, "The hat has jobs in it.
You can get a job from the hat and
help Mr. Grant."

Daniel said, "I'll take one.
My job is to clean the paint pans.
I'll clean the paint pans for
Mr. Grant."

Sam said, "Mr. Grant will like
the clean paint pans."

Mr. Grant said, "What a good job.
I like the clean table and the
clean paint pans."

Sam said, "I want to get a
job from the hat."

Mr. Grant said, "I'll put one into
the hat for you."

Sam read what Mr. Grant put into
the hat.

Sam.
Your job is to keep your hat here.
It is like you.
It is a big help.
      Mr. Grant

WATERMELON

PEPPER

Who Will Help?

Little Red Hen

One day Little Red Hen said,
"I want Pig to help clean the
house.
But Pig will not help.
Pig wants to play with Duck.
I have to clean the house."

Little Red Hen said, "I want
Duck to help out here.
But Duck will not help.
Duck wants to play with Pig.
So this is my job."

Little Red Hen said, "I have some wheat seeds here.
Pig and Duck and I can plant the seeds and make bread from the wheat.
Pig and Duck will like the wheat bread."

Then Little Red Hen said to
Pig and Duck, "I have some
wheat seeds.
Who will help plant the seeds?"

"Not I," said Pig.

"Not I," said Duck.

Little Red Hen said, "Then I
will plant the seeds."

And so she did.

One day Little Red Hen asked,
"Who will help water the
wheat plants?"

"Not I," said Pig.

"Not I," said Duck.

Little Red Hen said, "Then I
will water the wheat plants."

And so she did.

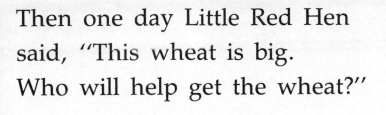

Then one day Little Red Hen
said, "This wheat is big.
Who will help get the wheat?"

"Not I," said Pig.

"Not I," said Duck.

Little Red Hen said, "Then I
will get the wheat."

And so she did.

Little Red Hen asked, "Who
will help take this wheat to the
mill?"

"Not I," said Pig.

"Not I," said Duck.

Little Red Hen said, "Then I
will take this wheat to the mill."

And so she did.

Little Red Hen asked, "Who will help make the wheat bread?"

"Not I," said Pig.

"Not I," said Duck.

Little Red Hen said, "Then I will make the bread."

And so she did.

Little Red Hen asked, "Who
will help eat this good bread?"

Pig said, "I will eat the bread."

Duck said, "I will eat the bread."

Then Little Red Hen said,
"No, you will not.
You did not plant the wheat seeds
and water the wheat plants.
You did not get the wheat and
take it to the mill.
You did not make the bread.
I did it.
I will eat this good wheat bread."

And so she did.

To be read by
the teacher

Seeds

by Aileen Fisher

Seeds know just the way to start—
I wonder how they get so smart.

They <u>could</u> come up in garden beds
feet first—by standing on their heads.

They <u>could</u> forget if they should grow
like sunflowers, high, or pumpkins, low.

They <u>could</u> forget their colors, too,
and yet they never, never do.

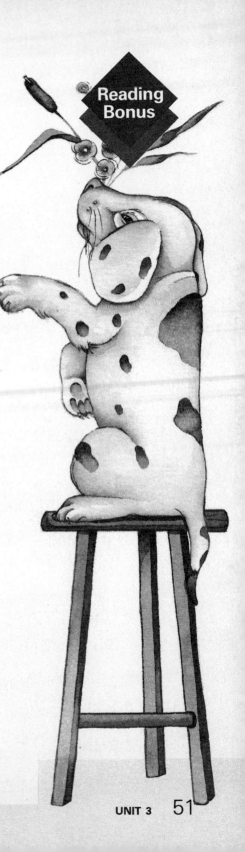

Help for Duck

One day Duck said, "Puppy, it
is good to see you.
I can not get up.
But I want to eat.
What can I do?"

Then Puppy said, "I'll get
help from Mouse and Frog."

So Puppy ran to see Mouse.

Puppy said, "Hello, Mouse.
Duck can not get up.
But she wants to eat.
You eat seeds.
Can you give Duck some seeds?"

Then Mouse said, "I have some
good seeds in this pail.
Take the seeds to Duck."

Puppy ran to see Frog.

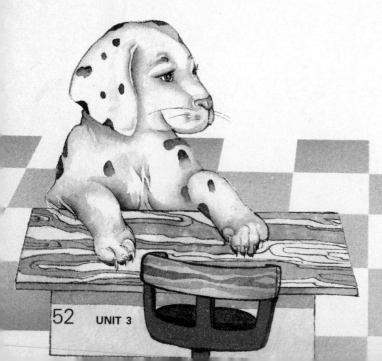

Frog asked, "What is in the pail?"

Puppy said, "I have seeds from
Mouse for Duck to eat.
Duck can not get up.
But she wants to eat."

Then Frog asked, "What can I
give Duck to eat?
Here is some good bread.
Take the bread to Duck."

So Puppy ran to see Duck.

Duck asked, "What is in the pail, Puppy?"

Puppy said, "I have seeds from Mouse and bread from Frog."

Duck said, "What a good job you did, Puppy."

Then Puppy said, "So did you, Duck.
Do you see what I see?
Here come your little ducks!"

Good Days

I Like This Book

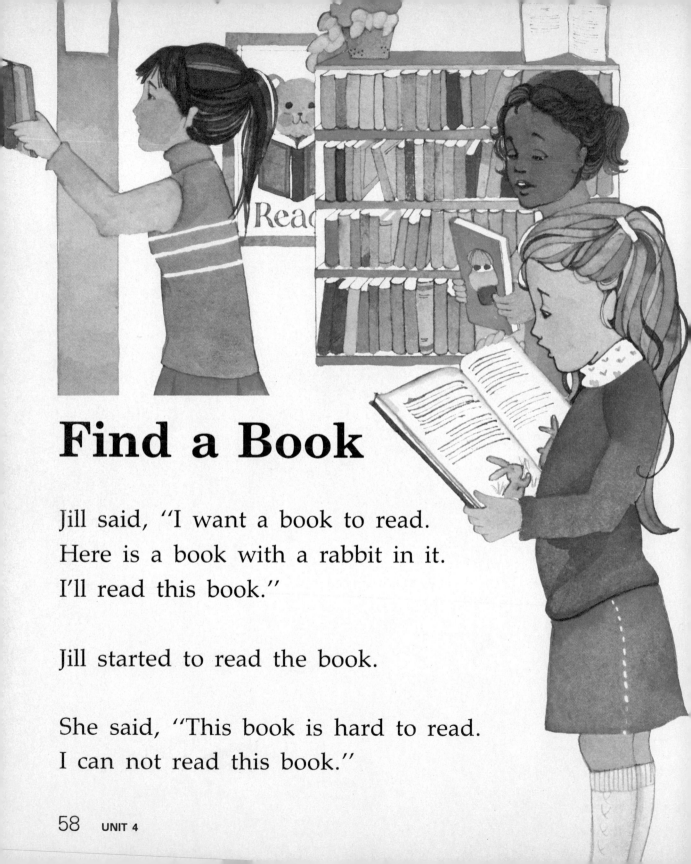

Find a Book

Jill said, "I want a book to read.
Here is a book with a rabbit in it.
I'll read this book."

Jill started to read the book.

She said, "This book is hard to read.
I can not read this book."

Jill saw a book with a turtle in it.
She started to read the book.

Jill said, "This book is as hard to
read as the rabbit book.
I can not read this book.
What can I read?"

Jill saw Ed with the rabbit book.

She said, "Ed, the book you have is
hard to read.
I want to read books like the one
you have.
What can I do?"

He said, "Jill, you have just
started to read.
You have to read and read.
Then you can read books like this."

Ed said, "Come here, Jill.
You will find books to read here.
This book is The Little Red Hen.
It is a good book."

Jill started The Little Red Hen.

She said, "I like this book.
It is not hard to read.
I'll read The Little Red Hen."

Jill said, "Ed said to read and read.
I'll get a book to take out."

Then Jill saw a book on the table.

She said, "This book is <u>The Rabbit</u>
<u>and the Turtle</u>.
The rabbit book is hard to read.
The turtle book is hard to read.
Is this book with a rabbit and a
turtle hard to read?
I'll see what it is like."

Jill started to read The Rabbit and the Turtle.

She said, "I like this book.
It is not hard to read.
Rabbit is fast, but Turtle is not.
This makes Rabbit laugh.
I want to see what Turtle will do.
I'll take this book out.
This is a book I can read."

The Rabbit and the Turtle

Rabbit said, "I am fast.
I can run.
You can not run, Turtle.
You just walk.
You make a rabbit laugh."

Turtle said, "Do you see the lake?
I'll get to the lake as fast as you."

Rabbit said, "What a laugh, Turtle.
You can not get to the lake as fast
as I can."

Rabbit started to run to the lake.
Turtle started to walk.

Rabbit said, "I am fast.
I'll stop here and go to sleep.
Then I'll run to the lake."

Turtle saw Rabbit stop.

Turtle said, "I am not fast.
But I will not stop.
It is hard for a turtle to walk fast.
But I will do it."

Mouse saw Turtle.

Mouse said, "Rabbit is fast.
He will get to the lake."

Turtle said, "No, Mouse.
I just saw Rabbit stop.
He wants to sleep.
I am not fast, but I want to get to
the lake.
I will not stop and sleep."

Frog saw Turtle.

Frog said, "Rabbit is fast.
He will get to the lake."

Turtle said, "No, Frog.
I saw Rabbit stop.
He will just sleep.
I am not fast, but I'll get to
the lake."

Just then Rabbit saw Turtle.

Rabbit said, "I'll run to the lake as
fast as I can."

Turtle said, "Rabbit is up.
He did not sleep long.
I'll walk to the lake just as fast as
I can."

Rabbit ran to the lake.
He saw Turtle in the water.

Turtle said, "You can run fast,
Rabbit.
But you stop and sleep.
I have to walk and walk.
But I do not stop.
So I am here in the water."

Just for You

You can make a turtle like this one.

1. Get this.

2. Make the turtle like this.

A Call for Help

The Firefighters

Mrs. Lake's boys and girls saw
a firefighter.

Mrs. Lake asked, "Can we talk with
the firefighters?
We want to find out what they do."

"Yes," said the firefighter."
"Come in."

A firefighter said, "The firefighters
sleep here."

Sue asked, "Why do they sleep here?"

He said, "Firefighters get up and
go to fires as fast as they can.
Fires get big fast.
The firefighters can not let the
fires get big."

The boys and girls saw a long truck.

Joey asked, "Why is this fire truck
so long?"

A firefighter said, "It is a ladder
truck with long ladders."

Joey asked, "Why do you put up
ladders at fires?"

The firefighter said, "We go up
ladders to get into houses.
We put water on fires from ladders."

A firefighter put a hat on the door
of the ladder truck.

Carol asked the firefighter, "Why did
you put your hat here?"

He said, "I ride to fires on the
ladder truck.
I ride at this door of the truck.
I keep my hat at the door so I can
get on the ladder truck fast."

Mike saw a fire truck.

He asked a firefighter, "Can this truck help you at fires?"

The firefighter said, "Yes, this truck helps the firefighters get water to put on the fires."

Just then a call comes in.
Dr. White's house is on fire.
The firefighters hear the call.
They get on the trucks as fast as
they can.
The firefighters will get to the
fire fast.
They will put out the fire.

Joey and the Firefighters

Mother asked, "Joey, why do you
have your firefighter hat here?"

Joey said, "I am a firefighter.
Will you let a firefighter sleep with
a hat here?
A call can come in."

Mother said, "I see why you want
your hat.
I'll let you keep it here, but my
little firefighter has to sleep."

In Joey's sleep, he saw some
firefighters on a ladder truck.

One of the firefighters said, "Joey,
a call has come in.
We will let you help with the call.
We have to put out a fire at
Dr. White's house."

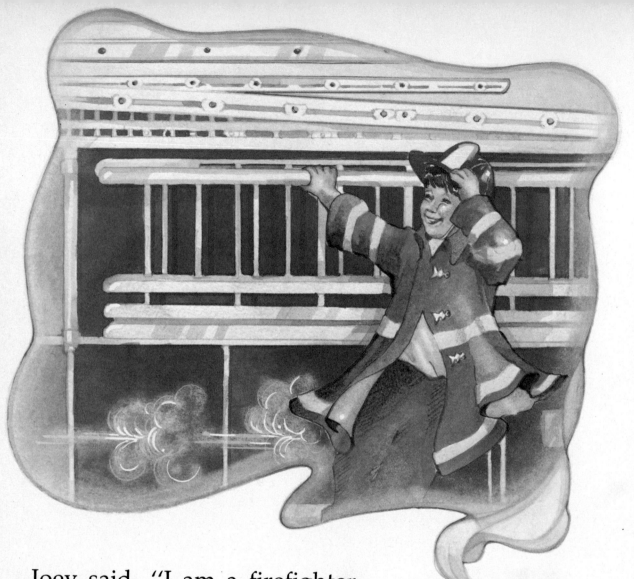

Joey said, "I am a firefighter.
I'll help you put out the fire."

Joey ran to the ladder truck.
One of the firefighters started the
truck.

At the house, Joey saw Dr. White
with Meg.

Dr. White said, "I started to bake
bread and a fire started.
We ran out of the house to call you."

Then Meg said, "I want to go into
the house to get my puppy."

Joey said, "We can not let
you go into the house.
A firefighter will get your puppy."

Just then the puppy ran out of
the house.
The firefighters put out the fire.

Mother said, "Joey is not up.
I'll get Joey.
I'll let Joey help make bread."

Then Mother asked Joey, "Do you
want to help make bread?"

He said, "Yes, I do.
But I'll keep my hat on!"

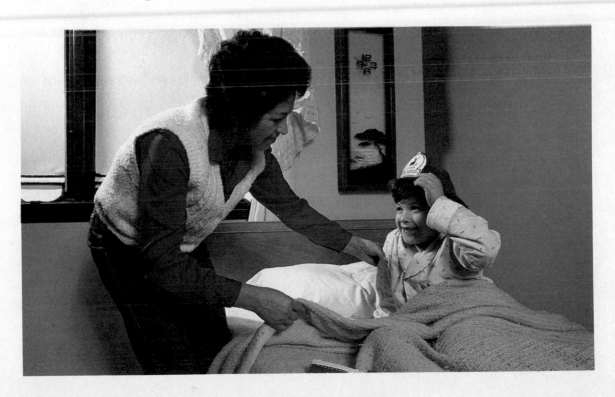

Play a Game

Red Light, Green Light

Carla said, "Mr. Long, can you help?
We do not have a good game to play.
Do you have a new game we
can play?"

Mr. Long said, "I have a good game.
I call it Red Light, Green Light.
Girls and boys, what do you do if
you come to a red light?"

"We stop," said the girls and boys.

Mr. Long asked, "What do you do
if you come to a green light?"

"We go," said the girls and boys.

"Good," said Mr. Long.
"Who wants to be the stop light for the first game?"

Carla said, "I'll be the stop light."

Mr. Long said to the girls and boys,
"I'll give this ball to Carla.
If Carla calls 'green light,' you can walk to the ball.
The first one to get the ball is the new stop light."

Mr. Long said, "Carla can not
see you walk on a green light.
Walk as fast as you can.

"Then Carla will call, 'One, two,
three, four, red light.'
If Carla has said 'red light,' she
can see you.
Stop as fast as you can.
If Carla sees you walk on a red
light, you will be out of the game."

Carla started the game.
The girls and boys started to walk.

Carla said, "One, two, three, four,
red light."

Then she saw the girls and boys.
Four of them did not stop fast.
So they sat with Mr. Long.

"Green light," said Carla.

The girls and boys started to walk.

Carla said, "One, two, three, four, red light."

Then she saw the girls and boys.
Three of them did not stop fast.
So they sat with Mr. Long.

Mr. Long said, "Just Bob and Judy will walk to the ball.
One of them will get it first."

"Green light," said Carla.

Judy and Bob started to walk fast.

Carla said, "One, two, three. . . ."

"I have the ball!" said Bob.

"Good for you," said Mr. Long.
"Bob is the new stop light.
Girls and boys, you can go and play
your new game."

What Can It Be?

Mrs. Lake said, "Boys and girls, it
is not a good day to go out and play.
I can let you play in the room.
But you can not run and jump."

Ken asked, "Bill, do you want to
play a game with me?"

"Yes," said Bill.
"We can play, What Do I See?
You can be first."

"Good," said Ken.
"What I see is in this room.
If we give it water and light, it
will get big.
What do I see?"

Then Bill saw the green plant.

He said, "If we give the plant water and light, it will get big.
Is it the green plant?"

"Yes," said Ken.

Bill said, "What I see eats seeds.
It is new to this room.
What do I see?"

Ken said, "The mouse eats seeds.
The mouse is new to this room.
Is it the mouse?"

"Yes," said Bill.

Ken said, "What I see is in the room.
It is good to eat.
What do I see?"

Bill said, "Mrs. Lake's apple is good
to eat.
Is it Mrs. Lake's apple?"

"Yes," said Ken.

Then Mrs. Lake saw Ken and Bill.
She sat with them.
She started to play the game.

"What I see is not in the room,"
said Mrs. Lake.
"It is big and yellow.
At first I did not see it."

"Is it a ladder?" asked Bill.

"It is not a ladder," said Mrs. Lake.
"What I see gives light."

Ken said, "One of the trucks is
big and yellow and has lights."

"It is not one of the trucks," said
Mrs. Lake.

"Let me see," said Ken.
"What can it be?"

Just then Bill sat up.
He said, "The sun came out!
It is big and yellow and gives light.
Is it the sun?"

"Yes, I see the sun," said Mrs. Lake.
"You can go out to run and jump!"

Jump with Me

Ann saw Jay and Beth play.

"I want to jump with them," said Ann.

But Ann just sat and sat.

Then Jay asked, "Ann, will you jump?"

Ann said, "I can not jump."

Beth said, "Jay and I will help you."

Ann ran to play with them.

Beth said, "I'll jump first so Ann
can see what to do.
One, two, three, four, jump!"

Jay said, "One day, day, day,
Frog came, came, came,
to play, play, play,
a game, game, game.

Jump, Frog, Frog, Frog,
said Beth, Beth, Beth,
the same, same, same,
as me, me, me.

Said Frog, Frog, Frog,
Beth can, can, can,
jump fast, fast, fast,
I see, see, see."

Then Jay said, "You go, Ann.
Jump in."

Ann said, "I can not jump in."

Jay said, "We will let you walk in."

"Good," said Ann.

Beth said, "One, two, three, four."

Ann started to jump.

Beth said, "One day, day, day,
  Ann came, came, came,
  to play, play, play,
  a game, game, game."

Ann said, "I can do it!
I can jump!"

Teddy Bear, Teddy Bear

Teddy Bear, Teddy Bear, turn around.
Teddy Bear, Teddy Bear, touch the ground.
Teddy Bear, Teddy Bear, shine your shoe.
Teddy Bear, Teddy Bear, that will do.
Teddy Bear, Teddy Bear, go upstairs.
Teddy Bear, Teddy Bear, forget your cares.
Teddy Bear, Teddy Bear, turn out the light.
Teddy Bear, Teddy Bear, say good night.

Good night!

Here Come the Animals

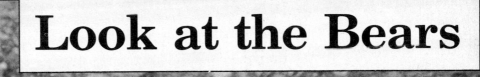

Look at the Bears

Big and Little Bears

The mother **bear** was walking with
the two little bears.
The little bears saw some cold water.
They wanted to play in the water.
The mother bear stopped to let them play.

The little bears play in the water.
They sit up and look at the mother.
She is getting into the cold water.
The little bears want to find out
what she is going to do.

The mother bear looks for a fish.
When she sees a fish, she takes
it right out of the cold water.
Then she eats the fish.

When the little bears want fish, the
mother bear gets some for them.
The little bears like eating fish.

The mother bear finds plants to eat.
The little bears like eating the
plants she finds.

The days go fast for the mother
bear and the little bears.

Then the days start to get cold.
When the days get cold, the bears
go to sleep.
They sleep as long as it is cold out.

When spring comes, the bears get up.
In the spring, the mother bear
helps the little bears find water.
In the spring, she helps them find
fish and plants to eat.

But one day the little bears will be
big bears too!
The mother bear will stop helping
them when they get big.

The Three Bears

One spring day Mother Bear said,
"Come and eat this good, hot fish."

Father Bear said, "My fish is too
hot to eat."

Baby Bear said, "My fish is too hot."

Mother Bear said, "It is spring.
We will go out for a walk.
Then we will eat the fish."

A girl called Goldilocks was going
for a walk the same spring day.
Goldilocks stopped at the house of
the three bears.
When Goldilocks saw the hot fish on
the table, she wanted some.
So Goldilocks walked into the house.

It was not right for Goldilocks to
walk into the house.
The three bears did not ask
Goldilocks to come in.

Goldilocks started to eat Father
Bear's fish.
But it was too hot.

She started to eat Mother Bear's
fish.
But it was too hot.

She started to eat Baby Bear's fish.
It was just right.

Goldilocks wanted to sit in a chair.
She sat in Father Bear's chair.
But it was too big.

She sat in Mother Bear's chair.
But it was too big.

She started to sit in Baby Bear's
little chair.
It was just right.
But look what she did to the chair!

119

Then Goldilocks wanted to sleep.
She jumped into Father Bear's bed.
But it was too hard.

She jumped into Mother Bear's bed.
But it was too hard.

She jumped into Baby Bear's bed.
It was just right.

Just then the three bears came in.
The house did not look right to them.
They looked at the fish on the table.

"Who was eating my fish?" asked
Father Bear.

"Who was eating my fish?" asked
Mother Bear.

"Who was eating my fish?" asked
Baby Bear.
"Look, I have no fish!"

The three bears looked at the chairs.

"Who was sitting in my chair?" asked
Father Bear.

"Who was sitting in my chair?" asked
Mother Bear.

"Who was sitting in my chair?" asked
Baby Bear.
"Look, I have no chair!"

The three bears looked at the beds.

"Who was sleeping in my bed?" asked
Father Bear.

"Who was sleeping in my bed?" asked
Mother Bear.

"Who is sleeping in my bed?"
asked Baby Bear.

Then Goldilocks saw the three bears.
She jumped out of Baby Bear's bed
and ran right out of the house!

Look at the Elephants

A Big Animal

Elephants are big animals.
Animals this big need to eat and eat.
Elephants eat plants.

Elephants can eat all the plants
where they are in one day.
Then they have to start walking.
They go where they can find new
plants to eat.

Elephants need water too.
They are good at finding water.
When elephants find water, all the
animals can come and get the
water they need.
This helps all the animals.

On hot days all elephants need to
be by water.
The elephants here went into
the water.
Going into the water keeps them
from getting too hot.

Some elephants are old, old elephants.
They can not walk fast.
Some elephants help the old
elephants by walking with them.
This helps the old elephants find
water and plants to eat.

A mother elephant helps its baby.
A mother elephant gives its baby
what it needs to eat.

When a baby elephant can not find
its mother, an elephant will take
on the job of being its mother.

Baby elephants help big elephants.
Baby elephants help by walking fast
when the elephants go where they
can find water and new plants to eat.

Time to Eat

Dad said, "Here we are at the zoo."

Tom asked, "Where can we get a pizza?"

"It is not time to eat," said Dad.
"I want to see the animals first."

So Tom and Dad went into the zoo.

When Do The Animals Eat?

10:00 bears

10:30 turtles

11:00 baby animals

"Look at this, Tom," said Dad.
"Here are the times the animals eat.
I like to see the animals eating."

Tom said, "All of the animals in
the zoo can eat, but I can not eat."

Dad said, "It is time for the
bears to eat.
Where are the bears?"

Tom and Dad went to find the bears.

Dad said, "I see a big bear."

"Is it eating pizza?" asked Tom.

"The bear is eating its fish, apples, bread, and green plants," said Dad.

Dad said, "By the time we find the turtles, they will be eating. Where are the turtles?"

Tom and Dad went to find the turtles.

Tom said, "The turtles are right
by the lake.
They look like old, old turtles.
One big turtle is eating its plants.
But it wants a pizza."

Dad said, "Pizza is good for you.
But it is not good for the animals.
We can go see what is good for the
baby animals to eat.
It is time for them to eat."

Tom and Dad went into the zoo for
baby animals.

Tom looked at the animals in the
zoo for baby animals.

"All the animals here are eating.
I need to eat too," said Tom.

"All right, Tom," said Dad.
"We can go get a pizza."

Tom and Dad went to get a pizza.

Tom asked, "Can we eat the pizza by the elephants?"

"Yes," said Dad.

"This is a good pizza," said Tom.

Just then an elephant went up to Tom.

"Look at the elephant," said Dad.
"It wants your pizza."

Tom said, "No, Elephant.
I have wanted this pizza for a long
time, and you can not have it.
Pizza is not good for you.
Here come your plants.
They are good for you.

"I like this zoo, Dad," said Tom.
"Can we see all of the animals?"

"All right, Tom," said Dad.
"But first I want to eat my pizza."

The Animal Song

Alligator, hedgehog, anteater, bear,
Rattlesnake, buffalo, anaconda, hare.

Bullfrog, woodchuck, wolverine, goose,
Whippoorwill, chipmunk, jackal, moose.

Mud turtle, whale, glowworm, bat,
Salamander, snail, and Maltese cat.

Polecat, dog, wild otter, rat,
Pelican, hog, dodo, and bat.

House rat, toe rat, white deer, doe,
Chickadee, peacock, bobolink, and crow.

Just for You

1. What time is it when an elephant sits in a chair?

2. What keeps an apple from looking like an elephant?

3. What do you call an elephant with four hats on?

1. It is time to get a new chair.

2. An apple is red.

3. Call the elephant what you like.
   But an elephant can not
   hear you with four hats on.

The Zoo for Baby Animals

Pat and Mom walked in the zoo for
a long time.

Then Pat said, "I like the zoo.
But I want to have an animal I can
keep in my room all the time.
I want it to sleep by my bed when
I am sleeping.
One day can we get an animal to
keep?"

"We will see," said Mom.

BABY ANIMALS

"Here is the zoo for baby animals.
This is where some of the baby
animals are," said Mom.

"Can I play with them?" asked Pat.

"Yes," said Mom.

Mom and Pat went into the zoo for
baby animals.

"Here comes a mother cat with four
baby cats," said Mom.

Pat said, "The cats like me.
Can we get a cat, Mom?
It can sleep by my bed."

"No," said Mom.
"Dr. Jones said I can not be in the
same house with a cat."

Mom said, "Here comes a man with plants for the baby rabbits to eat."

Pat asked, "Mom, will you be all right if we get a rabbit?
A rabbit can sleep by my bed."

"No, Pat," said Mom.
"I can not be in the same house with a rabbit."

Pat said, "Here are some baby
ducks by the water.
I like them, Mom.
Will you be all right with a duck?"

"Yes," said Mom.
"But when it gets big, it will not
like being in your room all the time.
It will not sleep by your bed."

Mom said, "Look Pat, this zoo has some fish."

"I like little fish," said Pat.
"Will you be all right if we have little fish in the house?"

"Yes, I will," said Mom.

"I can keep fish in my room.
Fish can sleep by my bed!" said Pat.

Books to Read

Are You My Mother?
by P. D. Eastman

A baby bird wants to find out
who its mother is.
The baby bird asks all the
animals it sees, "Are you
my mother?"

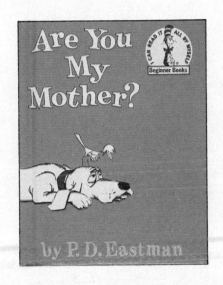

Just Like Daddy
by Frank Asch

You will read what a little bear
can do to be just like daddy.

Pictionary

Animals

cat
A <u>cat</u> likes to play.

duck
A <u>duck</u> can fly.

fish
A <u>fish</u> has to be in water.

frog
A <u>frog</u> likes to be in water some of the time and out of water some of the time.

pig

A <u>pig</u> likes to be clean.

puppy

A <u>puppy</u> likes to run and play.

rabbit

A <u>rabbit</u> eats plants.

turtle

A <u>turtle</u> is fast in water.

Things

bed

You can sleep in a bed.

bread

You can make bread and eat it.

chair

You can sit in a chair.

game

You can play a game.

ladder

You can go up a ladder.

pail

You can put water into a pail.

seed

A plant can start from a seed.

truck

You can ride in a truck.

Ways to Do Schoolwork

1. Underline the word.

2. Circle the word.

3. Write the word.

4. Circle the picture.

5. Put an X in the box.

6. Fill in the circle.

Words We Use Many Ways

call

I'll <u>call</u> Joey.

This <u>call</u> is for you.

clean

I have to <u>clean</u> my room.

My room is <u>clean</u>.

fish

I like to fish.

I have a fish.

help

I need some help.

I'll help you.

15

plant

This is a green <u>plant</u>.

I can <u>plant</u> the seeds.

water

Here is some <u>water</u>.

I can <u>water</u> the seeds.

Word List

88–105

light
game
new
if
be
first
two
three
four
them
set
me
came
same

110–123

mother
was
cold

sit
look
fish
when
right
spring
too
hot
father
baby
chair
bed

126–142

animal
are
need
all
where
by

went
old
its
an
time
zoo

143–148

cat
man

LIEN ELEMENTARY SCHOOL
469 Minneapolis Avenue
Amery, Wisconsin 54001